THOUGHT CATALOG BOOKS

Happily (N)ever After

Happily (N)ever After

Essays That Will Heal Your Broken Heart

THOUGHT CATALOG

THOUGHT CATALOG BOOKS

Brooklyn, NY

Contents

1

If He Wanted To Be With You, He Would Be With You

Kim Quindlen

It's a hard pill to swallow. But the truth is going to heal your heart a lot faster than simply letting it break over and over until you finally face what you knew all along anyway:

If he wanted to be with you, he would be with you.

There are a million possible scenarios here. It's easier when he's an asshole – selfish, only thinking of himself, using you to make someone else jealous, using you in general, treating you poorly, crushing you thoughtlessly, whatever. But it's a lot harder when he's a good guy, and you still have to let him go. When he tells you that you're an incredible person, but he just doesn't feel the same way that you do. Or when he really likes you, but doesn't think you're the one. Or when he just doesn't feel as strongly as you do and he wants to be honest. Or when he can't seem to make up his mind and feels confused, which he doesn't yet realize just means that he's afraid of hurting you, that feeling 'confused' just a softer way of eventually saying 'no.' If he wanted to be with you, he wouldn't have had to make up his mind in the first place. It would just be an answer that he felt deeply in his gut.

But regardless, whether he's a wonderful guy or an asshole or somewhere in between, this is about you, moving on. Because no matter what the situation was, no matter how well he treated you or how much fun you had together or how well you got along, he doesn't want to be with you. And that's the truth. And that's going to be your life raft for the next several weeks or months, no matter how much you don't want to grab onto it. It is what is going to eventually help you come to peace with the end of your relationship, or the fizzling out of your fling, or the 'no more talking' after you guys spent so much time 'talking.' It is the truth, and as ugly as it is, it will be the only thing that can help you move on:

If he wanted to be with you, he would be with you.

It's easy to try to soften the blow. *He needs time,* or *he just needs a little space,* or *he's just afraid of commitment and I just need to reassure him,* or *he builds walls and it's my job to kick through them.*

But think about the way you feel about him. How easy and natural and obvious it feels. How you don't even need to question whether or not you should be with him, because it just feels right in your veins. How, even if you were scared of committing to someone or getting hurt or opening yourself up, you were still willing to do it, because your heart had already made up your mind. You wanted to be with him, so you were. The decision was simple. It really wasn't even a decision at all.

Now can you imagine feeling all those things but choosing not to be with him anyway?

That's why your heart is broken. Because he didn't feel those things. He didn't feel that same certainty that you did, deep in your bones. And you can't change that, and you can't fix yourself, and there's nothing you did wrong. It's just the truth. His heart didn't make the decision for his brain, because his heart is in a different place from yours. And that really, really sucks. And you just have to accept it. And that sucks even more.

Maybe you'll get over this in weeks, maybe months. Maybe longer. It will hurt, some days will be horrible and some will be okay. But the smallest of silver linings is this: you can let your heart break once – instead of breaking it a million times by convincing yourself that he's making a mistake or he probably misses you or you should call him. Love yourself enough to be hard on yourself:

If he wanted to be with you, he would be with you.

2

To The Boy Who Emotionally Destroyed Me

Stefanie Manzi

I want you to imagine this: a girl sitting on her bedroom floor, dry-heaving, her body convulsing with each failed attempt at silencing the sobs, banging her fists onto the ground as she tries to make sense of it all. Now, I want you imagine my face because that girl was me, and I was never good enough for you. I was constantly coming second to dozens of other girls. You made me feel completely worthless. You emotionally ruined me.

I don't hate you, though. Instead I want to thank you.

Despite it taking me months, I finally realized that it wasn't me not being good enough for you but *you* not being good enough for *me*. These words have resonated with me for some time, and I am constantly reminding myself that I deserve better than the distorted perception of love that was handed to me on a tarnished silver platter. I deserve better than being ignored, I deserve better than being manipulated, and I deserve better than you.

I know I'm not the same girl that was on my bedroom floor that night, because I would never give someone complete power over me where I lost control; complete power over me where I felt I was worthless.

I know you're a good person, but next time you ask yourself what it was you ever did to me, I want you to think of the girl crying on her bedroom floor.

I was consumed by nothing but negativity, and for a while I thought you were my only source of light. I was drowning, and every single day I woke up and hoped your hand would pull me up to the surface and save me. I was wrong. That night was the night I realized your hand was never there to save me, but instead there to push me deeper below the surface. The only hand I needed was my own.

You were my darkness and it took me too long to realize this.

I know you're a good person, but next time you ask yourself what it was you ever did to me, I want you to think of the girl crying on her bedroom floor. I want you to think of the girl that couldn't sleep because the nightmares were worse than reality, which had become her own personal hell. I want you to think of the girl who couldn't eat because she had no appetite from the anxiety caused by thinking she did something wrong. I want you to think of the girl who hated herself so much she had to force herself to get up in the morning only to crawl back into bed hours later. I want you to think of the girl who had countless silent breakdowns, hoping her parents wouldn't hear. I want you to think of all the things you never saw, all the things you never experienced, all the things that were kept hidden.

And now I want you to think of the person I have become, and I want you to know that I am thankful for you creating a monster. I'm no longer a monster, and I no longer have to force happiness. No more do I have to seek validation from others that I am worthy. I am thankful you were a part of my life, because you became the best and worst thing to happen to me.

I do hope you're happy, and just know I don't regret you. I would never wish for you to experience the same hell as me, I just wish you the same happiness that I can finally experience every day. Thank you for engulfing me in darkness, thank you for helping me grow, and thank you for pushing me further below the surface. **Too many great things have come from that darkness. Too many great things have come from you.**

3

This Is How I Miss You, Even When I'm Trying So Hard Not To

Lauren Jarvis-Gibson

I still miss you sometimes.

The feeling comes quietly while I'm sleeping. I go to bed unharmed, and I wake up with a stomach ache all over again. And there is a hole in my body, like a bullet had just shattered my bones in my dreams. It isn't until noon that I realize it's you who I'm missing.

And then I realize I have missed you for three years straight. And even though I didn't always know it, a part of me always did and always will.

Some days, missing you has been quiet, like a soft whisper every winter. Yet, I trudged through the snow like we used to, with new strides in my step. Missing you just felt soft, like snowflakes melting into my warm mittens. It didn't seem to last.

But other days, missing you has felt like a stampede of longing and wanting and hoping in the hot summer heat. And I am drenched with your scent all over me once more. And I am tired. Tired of longing for something that doesn't exist. Tired of wanting someone who has moved on. Tired of hoping you will change your mind.

Tonight, as I drink red wine and try to sleep, I wish you were here.

I keep googling things, asking for advice, looking for excuses.

I keep asking the Internet how long it takes people to get over their first love. When will the longing stop? When will the bullets stop shooting me down? When will I find peace?

Google doesn't help much.

I tell others I am okay. *No, I don't miss him. I tell myself I am okay. No, I don't miss him.*

But, maybe instead of googling things, we should all just write down our truths instead of trying to hide them. Maybe we should speak up instead of silencing ourselves in fear of being shamed. Maybe we should be true to ourselves for once.

So, here is my truth:

I miss you on good days, on bad days, on warm nights, and on cold nights. I miss you when the sun is about to rise, and when the moon takes the sun's place for the stars to cover the black sky.

I miss you when I watch people intertwine their fingers together. I miss you when I look at my dried out prom corsage. I miss you after I have dreamt about you and wake up in a sweat. I miss you when I don't even know that I'm missing you.

And I miss you with every ounce of energy that takes to write this all down. But I am so tired of this feeling. I am so tired of it all.

A few years ago, I gave you a journal. On each page, I wrote out why I loved you.

I remember reading it to you in that fancy hotel. You smiled.

Things are different now. Years have passed by. And for you, I'm only a memory.

You are miles away physically, and miles away emotionally. This isn't a love letter. This isn't a dramatic plea for you to love me again. This is just my reality, and my thoughts that are flowing out of me so fast that I can hardly take a breath.

And so I admit, I still miss you sometimes. Maybe I miss you all the time. But, this isn't a love letter to you. It's a letter for me, to remind myself to keep on healing and to keep on going. Missing you does not define me. It does not diminish me.

And it never will.

4

This Is How Heartbreak Changes With Age

Camila Perez

At 14, he'll leave you for your best friend. You'll be alone for the first time, trying to piece back the pieces of a heart so young and so afraid that it has no idea what's in store. You'll scribble shitty love poems on the margins of your notebooks, take up smoking for two days and hide in the little crevice down by the beach that you call your own. You'll watch powerless as the two people you were meant to care about the most drift away from you. At 14, you won't know how to rebuild yourself. This will be your saving moment.

At 21, he'll leave you because he doesn't want to hurt you anymore. He'll argue that you're both toxic and deserve people who won't poison each other's minds as much. You'll stop eating, stop moving. You'll skip class and ignore the phone calls from friends trying to lift your spirits with wine and meaningless conversations. It will seem like the end of the world, but the world always finds a way to start over. At 21 you'll feel like a broken heart can actually kill you.

At 22, he'll say it's not you, it's him. He'll tell you he wants to be alone, that he doesn't want to be tied down just yet. You'll hug and promise each other an equally blooming friendship that compares to the romance you both had. Two weeks later you'll find out he's dating someone else. He'd been dating someone else. You'll grovel and ask for a second chance, a chance to prove to him that you're better than anything he could ever hope to find elsewhere. You'll betray everything you told yourself you'd never do again.

At 23, you'll destroy yourself completely because it's the only way to start over.

At 24, you'll be the one who leaves. Not on purpose, not because things went wrong, but because the universe had bigger plans and the timing, as it usually goes in overplayed romance stories, was off. You'll trace your fingers along his spine and whisper that you'll miss him. You'll kiss him good-bye multiple times, hoping to freeze that moment in time for as long as humanly possible. He'll mumble a few incoherent words as you walk out the door with everything packed into a bag that seems light compared to the thumping in your chest.

At 24, the promise of a new love will hurt more than the passing of an old one.

5

How It Feels To Be The Girl You Didn't Pick

Natalie Harmsen

I was the girl who was always evasive, shy, and unattainable because of my standoffishness. In my head, I told myself it was because I was intelligent and intimidating, and I let this sweep over me, permeating my thoughts and clouding my judgment. Naturally, it was a nasty wake-up call to not be someone's first choice. So when I — the girl who avoids conflict and always calls the shots — wasn't in control of the situation, it left me stranded.

There's a quote by Johnny Depp that goes, "If you love two people at the same time, choose the second. Because if you really loved the first one, you wouldn't have fallen for the second." I told myself this was completely accurate. Why would you ever want to be anyone's second choice? It shows how much you value yourself and sets a low price on your self-worth.

But it's one thing when you are the one they choose. It's completely another when you're the one left out in the cold, peering in from the outside on what could have been. For those like me who wind up the second choice, we always feel as though it was something we did, didn't do, or could have done better.

My mother asked me: "Did you do something to scare him away?" And at the time I pondered it, deep down wondering if maybe I had been too open, or not funny enough, or simply too invested in my own life. But I answered her as defiantly as I could: "No of course not. Who knows?"

Maybe he didn't choose me because he only liked the idea of me. Maybe it's because he thought I was different and special, the kind of girl who makes your head spin, and you tell your parents about because there's just something inherently indefinable about her — something you can't put your finger on because she makes your stomach ache with butterflies. But then the more I opened up, the more you pulled away. Was I supposed to leave an air of mystery? Maybe she did. Maybe she's everything I'm not. I can't compete with that.

Everyone says you weren't good enough for me. On paper, I suppose it's true. Far too busy and detached for someone like me, who thrives on openness and communication with other people.

Someday the storm clouds will part and the sun will smile down on me, reminding me that I'm above this. Until then I'm learning how to dance in the rain, allowing the water to wash away the sting of your rejection.

6

This Is Why You'll Leave Me

Jennifer Zhu

You'll leave me because that's what all the other boys did. You'll leave me for a girl who doesn't make you doubt yourself. Someone who will tell you what you *want* to hear rather than someone who will tell you what she thinks you *need* to hear. You'll leave me because you'll grow to hate me.

You'll hate the way I pick my split ends. The way I pout and sigh. You'll find the way I coddle you annoying. You'll grow used to me. The sex gets stale. You'll leave because you're bored. You'll leave because that's how it's done.

You'll find my ideals too cynical, yet not cynical enough. I don't agree with all your opinions. I'm stubborn. I can't communicate well enough. You'll find me strange: me and my fairy tales. Me and my hell.

You'll leave because you thought I was different.

That maybe I was someone worthwhile. Full of interesting thoughts, ideas, and jokes. But you'll soon come to realize that

I'm just like everyone else. I'm full of mistakes. I'm weak, but I'm a good person. And you'll hate it.

You'll leave because I've never been fully honest with you. My indecisiveness will bother you because you think it's because I can't make up my mind. But the truth is my mind was made up the moment our lips touched and your eyelashes brushed against mine. If I was honest, all those times you asked for me to decide the when and the where, my answer would have been the same: now, here.

And when you're leaving, slowly pulling yourself out of my arms, I'll know it's goodbye. I'll keep my eyes closed, breathing uneven. You'll pretend not to notice. Noticing would mean you would care enough to ask, and you might stay. But we both know that I'm not good at talking when it comes to the important things. So we'll keep quiet as you throw on your clothes. My mouth will open, eyes still closed. I should say something, but I don't know where I can start.

Once you leave, I'll be the one who has to look at the closed door. Stuck in the bedroom of my apartment, not wanting to let go, but not wanting to hurt. I can tell you now, it's a place I've traveled to. And it's not a great place to be. I'll fall back into bed, never having uttered a word, listening to the pounding in my ears.

My heart will beat like it's missing something. Like there's nothing else inside of me.

You'll leave because I'll never try to make you stay.

7

This Is How I'm Going to Remember You

Holly Riordan

1. Some days, it'll be through tears.

I'll flip through pictures on my phone and stumble across one of us, one I must've missed when I was deleting your existence. I'll get rid of it like the rest of them, but I won't be able to get the image out of my mind for the rest of the day. Won't be able to stop the tears that cascade down the cheeks you used to caress and onto the neck you used to nuzzle.

2. Some days, it'll be with self-doubt.

I won't be able to stop myself from checking your Facebook, or at least your Instagram, and when I see you smiling with another girl, your heads pressed together to fit into frame, I'll doubt my own beauty. I'll be blind to her flaws and only see the nose that's smaller than mine and the lips that are bigger than mine. I'll hate myself for being me and hate her for meeting you.

3. Some days, it'll be with a smile.

A commercial will pop on that we used to make fun of and I'll burst out laughing when I remember the way you used to grab for the remote to mute it. Or I'll pass by the diner we'd visit every week and I'll smile as I think about the waiter who swore that we were the cutest couple ever. Those will be the moments when I actually believe there's some truth to the whole "better to have loved and lost than never to have loved at all" thing.

4. Some days, it'll be with a laugh.

When I hear about the embarrassing things you've done at parties from friends of friends, I'll actually find it funny that I was once stupid enough to date you. I'll wonder what I ever saw in you and be thankful that you're gone, so I have a chance to raise my standards.

5. Some days, it'll be with hatred.

I won't always give you the credit you deserve. I'll call you a jerk. An asshole. The "C" word, even. I'll daydream about slashing your tires and burning your photos and taking a baseball bat to your lying face. I'll force myself to hate you as much as I used to love you.

6. Some days, it'll be with hope.

I'll catch a glimpse of brown hair from across campus and

think it's you, that you've come to tell me that you're still madly in love with me and want to fix things. That we're not really over. But then I'll realize that tuft of hair belonged to a stranger, and that now you're basically a stranger, too.

7. Some days, it'll be with confusion.

You'll send me a happy birthday text and I won't know whether to respond with a simple "thank you," to talk about how much I miss you and want you back in my life, or to refuse to respond at all. Should I work on moving on or work on getting you back? I won't know the right answer.

8. Some days, it'll be while intoxicated.

Months from now, I'll go out drinking with my friends, thinking that I'm already over you. But the drunken me, the me with no boundaries or common sense, will reach for the phone to text you. Unless I actually go through with it, I'll have no recollection of how much I yammered on about missing you when I wake up the next morning. I'll go back to assuming I've already moved on.

9. Some days, it'll be with lust.

I'll see a sex scene on Shameless, and I'll think about how much I miss feeling your fingers grasp my wrists to hold them over my head. Or you'll pop into my mind while I'm under the sheets, fantasizing about the new guy I'm crushing on, and then I won't be able to shake the thought of you. You'll be all I want, and I'll have you again, just in my mind, just for that night.

10. Some days, I won't remember you at all.

I'll be focused on my job, focused on my chores, focused on getting ready for the big party I'm going to. I'll be so busy that you won't have a chance to infiltrate my thoughts. Eventually, those rare days when you don't cross my mind will become my every day. Eventually, I'll hardly remember you at all.

8

I Only Miss You On Sundays

Lauren Hurst

I do not miss you on Mondays.

When the morning breaks I am in endless motion. I let the world swallow me whole into its vortex of responsibilities. My coffee and heart are both their strongest on these days. My mind is set on checking off a bold string of to-do bullet points, and loving you never makes the list.

I am content with the things I have let clutter my life, so I do not have room to think of you today.

I do not miss you on Wednesdays.

In these afternoons I am restless. We nickname Wednesdays like they are nothing but 24 hours of white noise, tired eyes and blank stares. They are heavy traffic on the freeway, something we just need to get through, convincing ourselves we will be happier once it's over.

I no longer have the energy to think of how we met on this day of the week, or how it was possible that the tingling in my hands that night was not excitement- but a warning.

I don't wish to go back in time and warn your curious molecules of my wandering atoms, to tell them that apart our constellations were captivating, but combined they will be four years of combusting supernovas, beautiful and destructive. I don't have time to ruminate on how you broke my heart on three Wednesdays, or how I broke yours on four.

I like the calm insignificance that has become wrapped within all of my Wednesdays since you.

I do not miss you on Saturdays.

On Saturdays I breach the shining surface. I break the ribbon at the finish line, an underdog in first place.

I am kind to myself, I take time to notice things within me and things around me. I make a conscious effort to forgive myself for the mistakes I've made and for the vice's I've refused to give up, the ones that anxiously took your place. When night falls I dig loose change out of the tip jar on my desk and paint on mascara without a waterproof safety net. I surround myself with people who I love and we laugh with the kind of whole hearted happiness that scrunches eyelids together and burns deep in your belly.

On Saturdays, I innocently flirt with strangers and dance without purpose. I do not feel your name lurking in the liquor burning down my throat anymore, I do not double take faces in the crowd that slightly resemble yours. The urge to call you does not even float across my mind, in fact I can't even recall the 9-digit finger sequence that used to drop me at your doorstep all too easily. You no longer have any part of my Saturdays, and God that makes me so happy.

I have persistently kneaded you out of six days of the week, untangling you from each day like pulling clean laundry from dirty.

But there is something different about Sundays.

There is a stillness that makes room for your memory.

There is a quietness that welcomes you out from the corners of my mind, that greets the memory of you with a sad smile.

My bed grows three oceans wider and four arctics colder on Sunday mornings.

My limbs are entwined with sheets that start to smell like a fading version of you.
The sunlight slow dancing with dust through the bay window never seems to settle on Sunday afternoons. The foggy realities of why we didn't work out, despite all-consuming attempts, cloud my living room.

The monstrous hangover of your absence throbs against my skull with the kind of relentlessness that no drug seems to numb.

Sometimes my Sundays taste like salt water. Sometimes they sound like 39 seconds of the song you used to love. Sometimes they end with scribbled words in my notebook, surrounded by pages painted with pretty words that have nothing to do with you anymore.

See, I only write about you on Sundays.

And I will let myself, because there are only 52 Sundays in a year. I will pack the hurt into a suitcase that remains locked until church bells chime and Saturday night subsides. I will spend the other 313 days of the year free from the tight grip of reminiscence. I will fill my Mondays with memories of places you haven't seen, I will meet wonderful people on Wednesdays, I will try new and risky things on Saturdays.

I will build myself a life that does not know you, and for 6 days of the week I will be painstakingly free.

I read once that it is not about who you miss at 2 AM when you're lonely, but who you miss at 2 PM when you're busy.

When I got offered a new job, you weren't the first person I told. When I bought a ticket across the ocean you didn't pop into my head. I have stories your curious ears will never hear and scars your wandering fingers will never trace, and on 86% of my days, that idea no longer breaks my heart.

See I only miss you on the day that allows it. I miss you on a day that make forgiveness seem feasible, that encourages sacrifice and romanticizes weakness. I only miss you on the day that was built entirely for quiet whispers, skin on skin and tangled bodies. I only miss you on day that so wrongfully convinces me that there is something still here worth missing.

In some kind of cathartic way, I think I like your lingering memory in those 24 hours- so you can keep my Sundays.

Because even a fool knows that all Sundays have sunsets, and all sunsets melt into sunrises. Every night the world will spin and the clock will expire. I like to believe this is the universe's whispering promise to me, as he leaves you behind tucked safely where you belong, in 52 of my yesterdays.

9

This Is Where I Leave You Because I Deserve Better

Shelly Ruiz

We had everything. We had the perfect chemistry, we had the greatest laughs, and we just understood each other in a way that everything we did together was in sync. It amazed us how perfect things were, how our different personalities just came together to form a perfect union between us. We were infinite.

But you were a jerk to me. You broke up with me with no previous warnings, just with bitter silence and later with hurtful words. I know it wasn't what you really wanted, but you were not "ready to take care of someone like me." I dwelled on it for a year and a half.

Was I too high maintenance? Did I come off as superficial?

I was relatively successful for my age and had lots of hopes and dreams for the future, and I was ready to accomplish and reach them all: with you…I had no limits.

Until my world fell apart with that one phone call, and those three words no girl wants to hear: "I'm not ready."

What did that even mean?

I was hurt like I've never been hurt before. I had always been the heart breaker, breaking up with boys I didn't see a future with, and truth be told, giving them hope when there really was none at all. For the first time, I felt what I had done to so many others all my life. I felt shattered, humiliated, and deceived. But I accepted it. I took a deep breath in the mornings when I woke up without you, and pressed my temples hard when I wanted to cry. I was bitter. I was angry. I snarled à la Godzilla when someone said, "time heals everything." I didn't want time. And if I couldn't have you, I wanted an explanation—closure.

But time did pass. And I did heal. I was no longer angry and bitter but content and satisfied. I lived my life, and slowly accomplished the goals and realized the dreams I had shared with you.

Until you came back. Slowly creeping into my life through social media, cute texts of cat memes that I love, complimenting me ever so slightly. And then that wasn't enough, so you asked to see me. Maybe just get a drink? And so we did. I drove an hour and a half to see you. You were there, waiting for me. You were wearing a plaid shirt and everything came back: the chemistry, our great laughs, and you understood me as well as I understood you.

Then you kissed me. And for a second, I loved you again. Just as much as a year and a half before. You held my waist, and you bit my lip softly, like you know I liked. We listened to music in your car, head bopping to ridiculous pop that we oh so hated. I made you laugh. You loved me for that second, too.

And we hung out a second time. We watched our favorite saga, debating whether BB-8 or R2D2 had a bigger space in our hearts. You held me closer and prepared me for one of the saddest scenes, and you held my hand tighter when you knew I was about to cry. After, we kissed, and spent another hour just listening to music kissing to Indie rock. I loved you for that second.

And you loved me, too.

And then we hung out for a third time. With all your friends. They all love me. But this time, you weren't exactly cute with me anymore, as if you wanted to hide how you truly felt. You weren't inviting. You kept looking at me, as if reassuring me of how you felt, but nothing was said. Other girls caught your attention. Not necessarily that you were attracted to them, but I was put on the side. I didn't mind, and started talking to some older friends. The girls were naïve and irrelevant; I let it go.

I said goodbye but left without saying goodbye to you. As I was leaving, I didn't look back, because I knew you weren't going to come after me. I knew expectations almost never align with reality. And I drove away.

I listened to Beyoncé to empower myself and remind myself who I was; it seemed as if I had forgotten. And then I decided:

This is where I leave you.

This is where I leave your secretiveness and your inability to say how you feel. Your disregard for my emotions, and the disrespect towards my persona. This is where I leave our chemistry. It is where I realize that I deserve someone who loves me, someone who can say the three words that can change a girl's life forever. Someone who will be grateful I'm by their side, someone who will flaunt me to their friends. Someone who would realize there is no other girl than me for them.

This is where I stop. This is where I breathe.

This is where I leave you.

10

I May Have Lost You, But I Gained So Much More

Stacy Kirk

When you broke my heart I thought my world was over. I couldn't eat, couldn't sleep, couldn't get out of bed. I thought I would literally never get over you. A few short weeks later and I am one hundred percent, completely, and totally recovered. In fact, I feel better than ever. So…why was it so easy?

I always loved you with everything I had. I loved you more than anything I ever knew, more than I thought I was capable of. It was a feeling I never experienced before and never wanted to lose. But, part of me always knew you didn't feel the same way. I thought you just needed time, that you would eventually feel these same unexplainable feelings I felt for you.

I knew how important I was to you, you made sure I knew that, not with words but with gestures.

But I always felt like you didn't feel exactly the same things I felt, and I thought that was my fault because I loved too much, too deeply, and with too much of my soul.

I'd always felt more love towards anyone I ever loved than they could give back to me, including my own parents. So it was normal, and I was the weird one, I thought.

I accepted it because I knew you loved me as much as you could. And to me, that was enough. But, when you said the words, *I don't love you as much as you love me*," I knew that wasn't okay. Those words hurt more than anything in the world. But, why? I knew it was true all along. I just couldn't believe you said it out loud. I tried to reason with you. I tried to convince you, and myself, that it was okay, that I just loved too much and you loved me as much as he could and that was okay.

But you left anyway. You said I would understand eventually. You left me no home.

That was it for me. I lost the only person I ever loved. But being alone for just a few short days I began to see that you were right when you said you weren't being fair to me, when you said you were not able to give me what I deserved.

You were right.

And all of the sudden, I was happy, happier than I had ever been. I was free and open to endless possibilities in life. I realized that love is the most powerful and most important thing in the world. I deserve to be the most important thing in someone's world. The more I thought about it the more I realized that I am a powerful, deep, passionate lover and there has to be someone who will love me back just the same. I need someone who can tell me anything, talk for hours, sleep under the stars with me, and tell me they love me every single day. I should have realized long ago, that's what I deserve. That's what we all deserve.

And here's what you taught me:

You taught me what it's like to be in love. You taught me what it's like to love someone for everything they are, for their strengths and weaknesses, perfections and flaws. And you taught me that I am deserving of so much more than you would ever give me. You taught me to never settle for anything less than what I deserve. I became a happier version of myself because of you.

When you broke my heart, it was the best thing that ever happened to me.

11

16 People On What Made Their 'Forever' Relationship Fail

Becca Martin

1. "I was young and wasn't really sure what 'forever' meant."

– Sam, 22

2. "I tried telling myself I was happy with him and that things would get better in the future, but they haven't. I'm still with him."

– Kristen, 23

3. "We were in a relationship for a few years prior to me leaving for work, I was only gone a few months until I received the call that she wanted to see other people. It broke my heart completely, I still can't believe it."

– Ron, 28

4. "We got in a motorcycle accident. I lived, but he didn't. I'll never set foot on another motorcycle again in my life."

– Kavanagh, 23

5. "After a couple years of dating things just turned routine for him. He stopped being the person I feel in love with and I knew it was time to walk away. He made me feel guilty for everything and started to manipulate me. It took some time and confidence, but I realized there were better things out there for me."

– Alex, 27

6. "She lied to me. She was cheating on me with her ex and some other random guys. I was blind sided, but once I figured it out I knew I had to walk away."

– Xavier, 23

7. "We grew apart, the people we were when we were growing up wasn't the same people we were in our twenties and I think we both realized that."

– Leah, 25

8. "I wanted to move away for work and he didn't want to leave his hometown that we'd been living in for almost 10 years. I knew that I was going to resent him in the future if I stayed with him there because I wanted so much more for myself."

– Bridgette, 32

9. "She wasn't happy, but she didn't tell me. She just let the relationship go on with me thinking nothing was wrong. I was completely blind sided by the ending."

– Matt, 24

10. "She left me for another woman."

– Kevin, 28

11. "I didn't treat her how I should have. I took her for granted and everything she did for me. I still miss her, but she's happy now it seems."

– Shane, 26

12. "He was my best friend, but he was mentally abusive and I didn't even realize it at the time. He didn't let me do anything without him and if I did it caused a fight. He was extremely insecure and took everything out on me and made me always feel guilty. I really thought we'd make it, but then I smartened up."

– Sara, 24

13. "Our forever relationship was almost too perfect to be true. But we were both too young for anything serious, but time will tell, he will always be my best friend."

– Lila, 22

14. "I made her feel alone in our relationship. I didn't treat her like I should have because I was too wrapped up in my own life that I wasn't giving her the attention and love I should have. I blame myself everyday for letting our relationship fail."

– Mark, 30

15. "I cheated on him. I was being selfish and I let my emotions ruin everything we built up together."

– Brit, 24

16. "He wanted more than what I could give him."

– Mary, 22

12

I Still Miss You

Kendra Syrdal

There.

I said it.

I am not heartbroken anymore. *Really*, I'm not. I'm not just a girl saying that to convince everyone staring at her with inquisitive, intrusive eyes. I'm saying it because it's the truth.

Really. It is.

"I miss you. There, I said it."

I no longer find you to be a habit.

I do not instinctually think to call you, I don't have your number memorized anymore (261? Or was it 216?) and when something happens I do not find my right hand reaching for a phone to start typing away to tell you all of the details. You are no longer my emergency contact and honestly, I don't think I would recognize your voice in a crowd.

But still…

There are days, and there are moments, where all I want to

do is look over at you at smirk and roll my eyes. There are days, and there are moments where I know I'm being stupid but you would still laugh at me. There are days, and there are moments, where I feel like you would be the only one to understand me.

I can admit that there are times where I know that even though I may not be able to remember your voice, I still miss your laugh.

And I still really want to hear it.

"I still miss you. There, I said it."

I'm no longer empty.

I do not feel like I have a gaping hole shaped exactly like your torso in my chest. I do not watch the blood pulsate in my veins and see your lies flowing through me. I do not look for you to finish my sentences or to pick me up at the end of the day. I am not trying to finish anything because I'm complete.

Really.

I am complete on my own. I'm whole.

But even still...

I find my fingers looking for the ink on your shoulders to trace and my hands looking for you to hold at night. I find myself swallowing down your name when I'm on an empty beach and wish I had more company than driftwood. I hold myself back from saying, "He would have loved this" on summer nights.

I may be whole, but that doesn't mean there isn't room.

"I still miss you. There, I said it."

I am not waiting for you anymore.

I do not stay up at night, I am not sitting in my bed while staring at the door just picturing you coming through it. I do not watch the clock keep moving and feel disappointed when you don't. I do not save a pillow for you, there's no water on the nightstand going untouched, there is no chair in my apartment with a permanent dibs. There's nothing for you here.

This is a world that I created without you.

This is not yours, and I'm not waiting for you to claim your space.

I'm not hoping, not wishing, not looking, not praying. And I am most definitely not waiting.

Because I'm older now, wiser now. And I know there's nothing there for me.

I've moved on.

There is no but.

I'm simply not heartbroken over you anymore.

…

Except…

"I still miss you. There, I said it."

There is still a longing. I can pretend to ignore it, that it is simply a result of too many glasses of wine and ballads, but it's there.

And try as I might, I do not, *no*, **cannot**, deny it.

Because I think there always will be.

Because I still miss you.

And I think a part of me always will.

13

10 Simple Ways To Heal A Broken Heart

Nicole Polk

"I can't do this anymore."

The words still ringing in your ears, bouncing around until they land like a punch in the gut. You're immediately transported to a new world, one you didn't know existed before this moment. A world and life without your beloved.

It doesn't feel real. You pinch yourself to wake up from this nightmare, but you're still here, still spinning from this declaration, this revocation of love.

Warm tears stream down your face until you begin to sob, that terrible uncontrollable sob that leaves you gasping for air. You want to hide away, cry yourself to sleep, and somehow magically feel better tomorrow.

We've all been here. Or some variation of it. We've all had our hearts broken and stomped on. We've all turned over every moment of our relationship in our heads and wondered, "What could I have done differently?"

But we are now transported into a world where the love we felt is snatched away from us and don't know what to do with ourselves other than grieve and mourn our loss.

I recently read a book that briefly touched upon heartbreak and it's advice basically amounted to "go out with your girl-friends as much as possible." WTF? That's it? That's how I'm going to heal my heart? Most of my girlfriends are scattered across the globe. Going out with them every night isn't even a viable option.

How on earth do you turn off those kinds of feelings? What happens to love lost? How do you mend a broken heart? I decided to investigate how to mend my own shattered heart.

In previous breakups, I've just idly fallen into my own personal patterns of love lost. For me, I cry, I stay in bed, watch bad tv, eat cookie dough, and hide away from the people who love me. I mostly don't DO anything. I sit and wait.

Because time heals all wounds, right? Or does it? If time is a construct of our minds, do we really have to wait for the passing of time, something illusory to heal ourselves? Can we speed up the process of healing our wounds? How much can we control our healing through our actions and patterns?

So, instead of blindly falling into my patterns, I started to ask myself some questions about my habits. I'm looking at my patterns with loving curiosity, playing with them a bit, see-ing what is actually serving me and seeing what patterns are there strictly because of efficiency, because my mind, body, and heart are too tired for anything but pattern. And here's what I've learned…

1. Lean Into Sensation

Essentially, everything we experience as physical beings comes down to sensation that we label "good" or "bad". When I began to lean into the sensation in my body, asking what it had to tell me, things began to transform.

I asked where the pain lived in my body. I closed my eyes and imagined personifying my sensation. I described what it felt like in writing, how I had to remind myself to breathe and how interesting the absence of a thing – air and love felt so heavy.

I examined the tightening in my chest, trying not to label it good or bad, just simply as sensation. Human suffering is largely a result of labeling experience as "good" or "bad" and "right" or "wrong".

The thing about sensation is, it's always changing. It doesn't stay forever. When we shift our perspective of experience just being a temporary state of existence, it takes the charge out of it, just through the simple act of observation. In my experience, the sensation itself tends to transform faster the closer I look at it.

By noticing how heavy the absence of air felt, I began to fill my lungs with slower, deeper breaths and saw my entire being become a bit lighter.

2. Frankie Says Relax

Remember those t-shirts from the 80s from Frankie goes to Hollywood? Turns out those guys had a good idea.

While this might seem a bit contradictory to just observing sensation, this practice of relaxing your body has slightly different merits. We hold so much tension in our bodies on a daily basis, and it's even more amplified in times of high stress.

Make a practice of scanning each part of your body for tension. I like to start out lying down on my back and closing my eyes like I would for savasana. Take a couple of deep breaths, then try to contract and tense up every single muscle in your body at once. Hold this for a couple of seconds, then release the tension in your whole body. Repeat a couple of times. I find it helpful to see the contrast in how my body feels between the tension and the relaxation.

Then take it further by slowly scanning each part of your body from head to toe. Tense up an individual muscle group for a moment, then release it. Crinkle your forehead, and release. Squeeze your eyes tight, and release. Clench your jaw, and release. Press your tongue to the roof of your mouth, then let it hang loose in your mouth.

You get the picture. We all know we hold so much tension and stress in our shoulders and backs, but also pay attention to the little areas. Relaxing the smaller muscle groups, particularly in my face, often make the biggest difference in how I feel afterwards.

3. Move It

Rest is important in healing a heart. But I often place too much emphasis on it. Yes, I need to take care of myself with sleep and the grace of stillness. But I now believe it is equally important to move your body too. The medium of movement isn't important. Just move.

On day one I went to a yin yoga class. While technically moving my body, the demands of yin yoga are much less than say a spin class. Yin allowed me to stretch my body while still allowing me to feel introverted and my presence internalized which was all I could handle.

On day two I went for a four mile walk in the park. I kept my headphones on and didn't talk to anyone, but stretched my legs and got plenty of oxygen into my lungs.

This movement is helping me keep some momentum and energy for other aspects of my life I don't want to put on hold while my heart heals.

4. Reach For A Better Feeling Thought

This one can feel a little tricky. For starters, the thought of joy can feel so far removed from where you are right now. So, start where you are.

If you are depressed, what next best thing can you reach for? Depression is feeling hopeless, despondent, withdrawn. There isn't even any energy around depression. Happiness and love can feel like a world away from depression.

Can you reach for something that feels slightly better than this powerless despair? Perhaps hope? Or anger or rage? Most emotions have more energy behind them than depression. While anger isn't a place you want to stay in, it can also spur some movement.

What if each day you worked towards an emotion only one step in the direction you wish to move? Take a look at the Emotional Guidance System scale I created from Ask and it is Given below. Moving up by one emotion a day will put you in a pretty good place in not so long a time.

Joy / Appreciation / Empowered / Freedom / Love

Passion

Enthusiasm / Eagerness / Happiness

Positive Expectation / Belief

Optimism

Hopefulness

Contentment

Boredom

Pessimism

Frustration / Irritation / Impatience

Overwhelment

Disappointment

Doubt

Worry

Blame

Discouragement

Anger

Revenge

Hatred / Rage

Jealousy

Insecurity / Guilt / Unworthiness

Fear / Grief / Depression / Despair / Powerlessness

There is something else to watch out for here. In the midst of my profound grief, I have moments of genuine laughter when I hear something funny. The first few times it happened, I immediately felt guilty.

It was as if my feeling good in any way was a betrayal to my broken heart. My brain was telling me that if I feel good, it's as if I didn't value that relationship as much as I thought I did. Well, that is hogwash. That is my hurt ego talking. My relationship meant and still means the world to me. Let me be really clear on this point...

Feeling good in the midst of grief is NOT a betrayal to what you are grieving

If you're having a hard time reaching for a better feeling thought, try some visualizations. Stay away from thoughts about your relationship and love. They are very charged topics, so start somewhere easy.

Close your eyes, imagine the feeling of the warm sun on your face, and cool breeze on bare shoulders. Imagine the taste of your favorite meal on your tongue. Imagine your abs aching after a good belly laugh. Build on this feeling with experiences from your own life you can draw from. What in your life is full of ease and joy?

5. Surround Yourself With Reminders Of Truth, Beauty, And Love

I have a tattoo on my left arm that says "Love..." Inspired by a blog post called the Beauty of the Ellipsis, it serves as a reminder that love isn't a finished thought. It is always in motion, always evolving. Love for myself, my family, my friends, and those I've lost.

I have a maple seed necklace to remind me that in every moment I'm planting the seeds of my future. I have prisms hanging from my windows for an extra punch of color and rainbows on sunny days. I am slowly building a jungle in my house. I fill empty spaces with plants that remind me of life and vitality even on the grayest of days.

Fill your surroundings and life with little bits that remind you of what you know to be true, beautiful, and joyful. These needn't be grand or expensive, just simply things that resonate with you. Here are some ideas to get you started.

Flowers from Traders Joe's. Pinterest board filled with beauty. Follow an inspiring Instagram or Tumblr account. Make or find a mantra. Use Canva to build and print out inspiring quotes to decorate your space. Go for a walk and find the perfect rock to bring home. Find a new favorite scent and spread it around your house liberally. Buy new stationary. Treat yourself to a print from Etsy. Draw images or inspiring quotes with sidewalk chalk in your neighborhood. Find a local place to make a coffee or tea mug. Alternately, find one that strikes your fancy at Society6. Create an altar or sacred space and fill it with crystals, palo santo, and offerings. Spend time with children. Find reminders of your truth and joy.

These may seem to be trivial things that are only on the surface, but I find the more I surround myself with items that feel whimsical and magical in some small way, the more I'm able to remind myself of how I want to feel in each moment. They help me choose to feel joy and magic when I might otherwise choose grief.

6. Self-Care Saturday (Or any day. Or every day!)

We can be quite punishing to ourselves in times of conflict and stress, so take some time to really take care of yourself in some way.

We're all busy and have responsibilities, but if you don't take care of yourself first, your responsibilities can begin to suffer as a result. I'm more focused and productive when I've taken care of my needs first. I attend to my responsibilities in a bigger and better way when my cup is full, not empty.

There's a lot of room for interpretation here as to what self-care looks like for each person. While technically, all the suggestions in this article are a form of self-care, I want you to block off some time specifically for self-care, digging deeper into what that means for you.

Maybe it's taking a long, luxurious bath and spending time pampering yourself with tinctures for your skin that make you feel radiant. It might be spending a couple hours in an animal shelter cuddling with puppies and kittens. Maybe it's scheduling a hot stone massage. Maybe it's nourishing your body with vibrant healthy food you've cooked yourself. It might be taking a couple hours to read a book that's been sitting on your nightstand for months.

Tailor your self-care and turn it into a weekly or even daily ritual.

7. Invest in Yourself

I'm willing to bet everyone has something new they'd like to try if only they had the time, money, or excuse.

Here is your permission slip to try that something new.

Did you want to pick up knitting, or maybe learn to play the guitar? Maybe learn some knife skills to elevate your cooking? Rock climbing, sky diving, painting, learning another language, the possibilities are endless. You can find a class on just about anything you like online these days.

As children, we try new things all the time. It's how we learn and grow at an exceptional rate. But this slows down as we grow up and our field of vision becomes smaller as we narrow down our playing field. So expand your horizons, invest in yourself in some way, and learn something new.

The cognitive requirements of learning something new can also serve as a great form of distraction when you need a distraction. Maybe you'll end up picking up a new hobby, check off another box on your bucket list, or have a good story to tell.

8. The "F" word...Forgiveness

Ahh, a big scary one! The topic of forgiveness can be a novel in itself. Maybe you need to forgive the actions of your ex, or maybe forgive yourself for your own. Or a combination of both.

We don't always like to forgive people for actions we deem wrong or hurtful because it can feel like we are giving them a free pass. But I've learned that holding onto anger and resentment is always worse. It's a tremendous energy suck and you can't feel joyful as the same time you are feeling justified in your anger. So, I choose my own happiness over my resentment.

It's a choice to make over and over again. It's not easy to forgive in one big sweeping motion. It generally happens in increments. It's helpful to practice radical empathy, vividly imagining how it feels to be the person who did you wrong. You know most people are essentially doing the best they can with the information they have at each moment. It becomes easier to imagine why they did what they did when you put yourself in their shoes. You begin to feel more compassion for them.

You recognize that the anger you're holding serves no one. And you slowly begin to let it go, piece by piece.

Because forgiveness is not for them, it's for YOU.

9. Give what you wish to receive

I was walking around, feeling like no one loves me, which is totally and utterly false, but when you're heartbroken, your mind says all kinds of irrational things. I saw a friend of mine post about writing a letter of encouragement to a friend, and I wished to be that friend with every fiber of my being. I wanted to open up my mailbox and see letters of love, a validation of the love that exists for me.

I asked myself what could I do to feel that love? I decided to GIVE what I wished to RECEIVE. I started writing letters of encouragement and love to friends and strangers alike. All I had to do was write what I wanted to hear, for myself. It was that easy.

This did two things for me.

One, the brain doesn't distinguish between giving, receiving, or even witnessing generosity. When you perform an act of kindness, the pleasure and rewards centers light up, releasing feel good chemicals as if you were the recipient, which some psychologists have dubbed the "helper's high."

Two, it shows me that we live in a world of abundance. I don't need to hoard away love and kindness to keep it. It actually grows when I give it away. It's generative. And often, when you give love and kindness away, others are inspired to mirror your love and kindness back to you as well as pay it forward to others.

We cannot presume to understand the power of the depth of what a few kind words can do for someone and it's ripple effect on the world. Win win win!

10. Investigate Your Own Patterns

This is by no means a complete list. Merely suggestions of the beginnings of opportunities for your own healing. The biggest thing you can do for yourself is to get curious, examine your own personal patterns in the experience of heartbreak, and question each one.

Hold each one up as they appear and ask "Does this serve me?"

If the answer is truly yes, keep it. If the answer is no, try something new or the opposite of that first instinct. Play with the new reaction, see if that one serves you better, makes you feel better both in the present and the long term.

And most important, be gentle with yourself. There are times to push your boundaries, to examine, and to experiment. But there is also a time for rest and a time to surrender. Give yourself the grace to know you are where you need to be when you need to be.

Use this time to crack your heart open rather than an excuse to just be broken.

Know that you won't always feel like your heart has been ripped out of your chest. Shorten the distance between a shattered heart and a mended heart by experimenting with these alternatives to your patterns. One day you'll open your heart again and feel the rush of falling in love. You'll look into eyes that truly see you and mirror your soul back to you. And you'll be ready for big love because you've already done the work to heal your heart.

14

Everything I Wanted To Say (But Didn't) When You Broke My Heart

Alexandra Marie

get out of my head you fucking idiot. i hate you so fucking much. you made me believe that you actually liked me. did you actually really? /?/ was i not pretty enough. wasn't i good in bed. fuck you. fuck you so fucking much. you hurt me so fucking much. i've never felt as happy as i did when i saw you in the airport that day. happy and nervous. nervous but happy. and the way you leaned in the car, allowing your cheek to hit my lips as you subtly looked at the billboards that i will now loathe. it was an assurance for me that day, that i lived to your expectations — that i was allowed to touch your skin. and now someone else is touching yours. while your skateboard is still in your room in the house, like how i am right now in the middle of the dining room with a glass of wine that will last for one more sip. i wish i had more. i want to drown — but i don't know in what. i wanna drown and forget you. i wanna drown in you. i want you to magically appear at the front of our gate. i wanna take you around to my favorite never been to places. i wanna experience everything with you. i want to see your eyes in awe. i want to be the one to give you that. me. and no one else. i want to show you what beauty is for me, and secretly hope that you find beauty in them too.

i wanna forget you. erase my mind of every moment of you. because you're the fucking worst what could've been. i still think that theres something wrong in me, you fucker. never good enough. part of me thinks i am better than all the other people you're fucking seeing right now. more intelligent, more well cultured — but maybe thats not what you want. maybe you want someone who can dance with you and your stupid british rap songs that i find myself humming out of nowhere. maybe you want someone who has a smaller waist, slimmer arms, clearer skin. but i honestly thought you wanted more than that — you can see past that. it's so unfair.

you didn't give me the time you're giving them. you rushed yourself into me as i was rushing into you, but you made it move a light speed. you did a fucking grand gesture that i say i find creepy but damn fuck you because who else would travel thousands of miles for me? who? no one but you, you fucker. imagine me finding out that i wasn't enough after all. that you went here to be with me — and you found that theres so many things that you want to do other than be with me.

i hate thinking about who you're with. when i'm walking down the street — i think of who you're kissing. when i'm eating, i'm thinking about who you're saying all the filipino words to that i taught you — all those words mixed with your stupid charming accent. you know how to make them swoon — you've seen me be swept up.

you know the look i give you — you've pointed it out twice. one time when we were walking down and you said "ha, that look you give me when you want to kiss me." and yesterday when you said "stop it, don't try to kiss me".

the pause

you see, i can go all emotional ape shit on you and drown in my sorrows and heartache that your fucking self did to me

then all it takes is a pause

then i remember how much of a cunt you are — that you do not deserve my bittersweet words

that you deserve no limelight, good or bad

that i can move on, and be with someone who will love me fully, love my flaws, and fucking give me a tight hug, and kiss me afterwards, and cuddle with me til 10 am, and kiss my morning breath, and grip my hand super tight when we walk down the streets we used to walk down on, and will take me to all the places that remind me of you and will remind me again the beauty i once saw in that place.

i'll get over this, you, the miles, the billboard, the airport, the night we met and talked until 7 am. i'll get over one of my favorite trips with my friends where i took you with me through the lens of my phones. i'll get over your scent, your hair. i'll get over the night you said you're not ready for a commitment and the night you said you were ready — for someone else.

i'll get over this fucking stage in my life, because i'm only 20, it's only february, and there are other people who deserve the genuineness i gave you. the vulnerability. my heart.

it's still beating.

this is a heartache in words

this is how you think out loud, ed sheeran

fuck you

i'm free

my head is free

my heart is safe still beating

everything will be fine

or even better

15

10 Reasons Your Last Failed Relationship Isn't A Failure, It's A Lesson

Nicole Tarkoff

1. It makes you realize the love that you deserve (and who deserves your love in return).

Sometimes it's difficult to accept love, and sometimes it's even more difficult to realize that you deserve it. A failed relationship is an opportunity for you to recognize all the things your partner failed to give you, and all the things you gave them that they failed to appreciate. You deserve someone who doesn't take those things for granted, someone who appreciates the little things you do for them, and who does little things for you in return.

2. You learn what you do and do not want.

When you and your partner fail to make each other happy, you realize what it is you want that they never gave you. It made you angry when he never thanked you, and now you realize all you want is a decent dose of gratitude. It made you sad when she broke the promises she made, and now you realize all you want is loyalty. The disappointments you endured allow you to figure out what it is you truly want so that you'll never have to endure the same disappointments again.

3. You learn what you need from someone else.

Being in a relationship teaches you how to balance dependability. You find the line between depending on your partner, and allowing them to depend on you, and you attempt to manage both. And when either one of you fails to be dependable you realize exactly what you need from someone else that they just couldn't give to you.

4. You learn what you *don't* need from someone else.

When the relationship ends you quickly begin to realize everything you're capable of completely on your own. Solitude becomes something you appreciate rather than fear, and independence feels less like loneliness and more like an accomplishment.

5. You learn what you're not willing to give.

Flexibility is key, but for the sake of a relationship, there are some things not worth compromising. You shouldn't have to give up a part of yourself for someone else. If the relationship ended because you failed to do so, then you're better off without them. You learn that you need to find someone who accepts all of you and that includes what you can and cannot give them.

6. It allows you to acknowledge your weaknesses, and work on them.

Your partner made mistakes, but so did you, and while the failure of your relationship doesn't rest solely in your hands, the fact that it's over allows you to see what you did wrong. Maybe you were guarded, or maybe you let them in too fast, but you are now a little more familiar with the way you share your life with someone else, all imperfections included.

7. You learn that life doesn't always happen the way you imagined it would.

Maybe you thought you both would be together forever, or maybe you thought it would end sooner than it did. When someone you love unexpectedly leaves, or when the downfall of your relationship surprises you, you feel like life is completely out of your control, and at first it seems terrifying, but as more time passes the more comfortable you become with uncertainty. Because you'll never truly know if someone is *right* for you or if you're on the *right* path, and when things don't go according to plan this becomes not only more apparent, but more familiar.

8. You have time to be selfish.

When you spend so much time with someone else, it is natural to put their needs before your own, but when you finally have the time to be alone, your needs sit first row. It's okay to be selfish when you weren't giving yourself enough attention to begin with.

9. You learn that you're resilient.

Whether the end of your relationship was a mutual agreement, or a blind-sided betrayal, you survived, and you're still here, and whatever condition your emotions are in, you're still breathing, and you'll continue to each day. You learn that your heart isn't as fragile as you thought it was.

10. You learn that you'll be able to love again even after you've been hurt.

The same way you survived heartbreak is the same way you'll be able to find love again. Continue to live your life and do what makes you happy, and your last failed relationship will feel less like failure and more like something that helped you to move forward and let go.

16

This Is Why We Struggle To Leave Someone We Know Is Not Right For Us

Elizabeth Stone

Bad relationships don't happen all at once, they creep up on us. If they were bad in the beginning, no one would ever do it. So, why do we stay in bad relationships long after it dawns on us that it's time to go?

Here are three reasons why leaving a bad relationship is a lot harder than it sounds:

1. You feel like you've put in too much time to give up now.

Once we start a relationship and put in the effort to keep it going, stopping feels like we're losing our investment. The realization that we've wasted months or years of our life staying with the wrong person is often too much for us to come to terms with.

2. You want to be the hero of your relationship.

Sometimes we fancy ourselves as the other person's savior. We tell ourselves nonsense like, "They would be so devastated by the breakup that they would never recover."

Hooey. You aren't doing anyone any favors by continuing a relationship with them because you feel bad about telling them it's over. Yet, plenty of people stick around, feeling too much shame to admit that they are dying inside.

3. You make yourself believe that this relationship is what you really want — even though you don't.

This one is tricky. Confirmation bias (also called confirmatory bias or my side bias) is defined as, "a tendency for people to favor information that confirms their preconceptions or hypotheses regardless of whether the information is true."

What this means for relationships is that once you get into one, you will work hard to confirm that continuing the relationship is a good choice.

This natural tendency is helpful when we're in a good relationship because seeing the good helps us get through the hard times. Unfortunately, this is a disaster when we find ourselves in a toxic pairing.

In the honeymoon phase, we often tell everyone (particularly ourselves) how excited we are about our new mate. Then, as the realization hits that the other person is not good for us, we'll stick around for a while (sometimes a lot) longer in an emotional space of being unwilling to admit that we cut the wrong pony from the herd.

17

I'm Not Supposed To Still Care About You, But I Do

Amanda Cirocco

It's been a few weeks, and you haven't come around. I haven't gotten a late night text and I've been unable to sleep. You see, I keep waking up to nothing; thinking that one night, you'll have a change of heart — but I know. I know that it's settled.

So, this is it right? This is how it all goes. This is the destination I have so desperately wanted to reach and you're no longer here. You were never going to be; I was always flying solo.

Ironically, I have trouble making words of this — this nothing that has perplexed every bone in my body to become still. It's like diving into the Atlantic in the dead of winter I knew it wasn't right, but I did it anyway.

I lied to myself, and now I'm left with the hurtful truth.

But this is…hard.

This is…not fair.

This is….not how I pictured it.

This is…not what I wanted, because I really wanted this to work out.

But wants and needs are on two opposite spectrums and my want destroyed my need. It's never going to be enough, and I don't know who I'm trying to impress or have validation granted too — I guess I had these expectations that were not realistic.

I wanted to love you, and I wanted you to love me in the ways that you told me love is. Because truthfully, I don't know what love is. You've been in love, but not with me.

I don't know what it's like to wake up in someone's arms every morning, and feel a warm body pressed up against me.

I don't know what it's like to have fights and make up an hour after.

I don't know what it's like to have anniversaries and "first dates" or favorite restaurants that you spend hours talking in, realizing their closed and the waiter is standing by the door staring you down.

I don't know how to do this, any of it. And I don't know if what I ever felt was love, or just lack of. I don't know if my fascination and unrealistic expectations led me so far down the rabbit hole I never got out of it.

I thought I was going to learn but you weren't up for teaching.

I don't know anything about you, only a boy I thought I did. But that boy isn't you. We're not seventeen anymore. You aren't the boy I wish you were and I'm not anything that I used to be. It wasn't something. I was just that — nothing. We were merely just moments to one another — if that.

When I hear your name, I shut my eyes and even then I still see you.

When I see your name my body flinches, and I get chills, piercing ones that leave me paralyzed until I can finally come to my senses — until I can finally feel that you've given me nothing to.

You were the most unlovable human besides myself. And I know that now, this is how it all goes. You'll be the kid I tell my daughter about, the kid that will make you feel butterflies inside your stomach — but one day you'll have to let them fly. You have to let go of the people who were destined to go. She'll not know what it's like, until she meets your son.

You are not a bad man; you were just incapable of being a good man to me.

You are a good person, I'll give you that always, and you will be a good man to a good woman. But she won't be me. I don't know why it took so long, for me to get it. And you tried hard, to show me it would never be us. I'll never actually get it, though. Like you said, some things just don't have clear cut answers. I'll have to live with this, till I either accept it or it destroys me.

I tried to force two people who would never be magnetic.

So it's been weeks, and I miss you right now because I feel like I'm still hanging on to your magnetic strip, and you're trying to flick me away. There'll be a new magnet in town, down the road and I'll be here, still away at school.

I'm sure in several months or so, you'll be bored and wanting to feel that urgency I have always given you. Because that's who I was, the one to jump in my car the second you asked me to come by, no matter the hour, time was never on our side.

Maybe you'll have a way with words as usual and give me some speech, and I hope I don't respond because I'll just be continuing this vicious cycle that I hate myself for getting back on. It's not fair and it's not love — I don't know what it is, but I know what it's not.

I'm not supposed to feel this way about someone I wasn't in love with, someone who didn't love me the way I wanted to be. I'm not supposed to still care and cry and feel this way.

Can you tell me why I do? Could you do that, no you can't. I'll always want your validation, I'll always feel this thing for you, and it's the one thing I have that you don't. You can't take this away from me no matter how much it destroys me.

18

Why The Worst Breakups Are The Best For Moving On

Tatiana Pérez

You just stormed out of his place, screaming, cursing his life, swearing you hate his dumb, selfish guts. It's over, and the end was *not* pretty. In fact, it was super fucking heinous.

You're reeling. You just lost your shit. Like… someone. Please. Help this girl (you) locate her shit, because it is LITERALLY nowhere to be found. You made a scene, and you feel like the most veritably psycho bitch on the planet.

You're not crying (yet). You're on your way home, immobile, staring at your phone, not knowing where to start. Who to text. What to say. You're in shock. Did you really say that? Did *he* really say that? Did the neighbors hear? You're clueless. You've never had an out-of-body experience, but tonight was distressingly close. Bitch, you need to *breathe*.

You did really say that. So did he. It was… ugly. You loved each other. Shit, you probably still do. You don't want him to have a miserable life. You don't hate him. And now your regret is giving you acid reflux.

"FUCK. ME. WHY DID IT HAVE TO END LIKE THAT?" That "good" breakup of your tear-soaked dreams is not your reality. Good.

You have this lovely, romantic idea of what a "good" breakup might look like. You'd wish each other the best after having beautifully tragic breakup sex. He'd kiss you and whisper something whimsically nauseating like, "I'll always love you." You'd leave a perfect, pink diamond-encrusted key to your heart on his bedside table. He'd always look for your scent on other women. It'd be fucking poetic.

But that poem, as pretty as it is, is a joke. That "good" breakup of your tear-soaked dreams is not your reality. Good. Because if you think exploding into a thousand *I hate you*s for one shitty night is hard... well, it is. It's brutal. But worse still? Breaking up with someone without really breaking up, at all. Having a breakup so amicable, so sweet, so loving, that you can't *move the fuck on*.

Untie yourself from him. Say "fuck you," even if you don't hate him, because yeah, FUCK him. Fuck him, fuck your breakup, fuck it all. Fuck the way you treated each other in the end. And *fuck* being "crazy" in love. You were wild for him, and when it started to crumble, all you could do was gape at the ruins of your relationship in furious disbelief. Fuck that.

Now, you've gotta do the only thing there is to do: *You.*

You've got to take all that rage you felt towards him in the *final hours* and turn it into something productive for *you*. You've got to laugh, because let's face it: That breakup was fucking hilarious. Bravo should've been up in that bitch with a full camera crew and Andy Cohen on call to *unpack* the drama with you. And then you've got to start a new chapter of your bomb ass life. You don't want to feel all those gooey attachments a "good" breakup would've engendered. Trust. You want to feel vindicated by your anger, and you want to keep it moving.

Fuck him, babe. Something good is happening.

19

This Is Why You Can't Keep Wondering What You Did Wrong After A Failed Relationship

Elizabeth Stone

I'm not proud to admit it but after one breakup, I was completely stuck on the idea that my ex didn't like my hair color. This sounds ridiculous, but stay with me.

I built this up in my mind to be a big part of the reason we broke up. I was 100% willing to ignore the fact that we were totally incompatible and deep down, didn't really have chemistry.

Instead, I got totally stuck on hair color. As embarrassing as that is to admit, it's a big mistake that people make after breakups.

If you've never been prone to dwelling on the past, or trying to get closure this might not resonate with you. From my experience with coaching people through their breakups, it's common to get stuck on a few weird things that could have changed everything if you had just done them differently.

Often when people contact me to find out where their relationships went wrong, or how they drove someone away, they are really trying to figure out if whatever it is that they are stuck on was the real reason for the breakup.

It's as though they believe knowing the past real reason will change something about the present reality.

At some point they decided that they messed up.

Most of the time, they are going through a bunch of what-ifs.

They ask themselves questions like:

- Should I have said something different at a specific time?
- If I had had "the talk" would that have made them commit?
- Was my hair, body, outfit the real reason we broke up?

The desire to figure out what we did wrong is healthy and helps our growth in the long run. Letting your imagination run wild while coming up with reasons that your ex left or a promising date went badly, is not.

Unfortunately dwelling on any part of a breakup is an exercise in futility.

Even if you did figure out the correct, non-polluted, totally true reasons why the breakup occurred, it still doesn't change the reality. You can't go back. You can't use the realization to rewind back to the start of your relationship.

And you shouldn't want to.

Why?

Every relationship experience contains a lesson. Either the person was for you or wasn't, but getting to the point of breakup means that both people have something to learn. These lessons likely weren't trivial or specific moments where one person said the wrong thing.

When a relationship starts to go badly, it erodes over time. Relationship conflict doesn't happen because of any specific, one-off thing. It really does take two to bring a relationship down.

This is why it's likely that if you're stuck on what you said, or not being blonde or anything else, you miss the real, bigger picture reason that it didn't work out which could actually help your growth.

For conversation's sake, maybe you DID drive them away. Maybe you were a total jerk. However, there is a difference between beating yourself up with hindsight and calmly recognizing your part, resolving to change and moving on (whether you try and patch it up with them or not).

The obsession with the what-ifs is not healthy or helpful. It also serves as a powerful temptation to keep you stuck in the past. If you are focused on the past, it makes it pretty darn hard to move forward in the present. Most of the time, the obsession serves as a placeholder for rational self-examination.

The lesson gets lost while you're beating yourself up. You might have big regrets, and these might make complete sense, given the circumstances.

I know I've stepped away from a few relationships thinking, "wow... I messed that up pretty monumentally" (and this is honest. I do mess up monumentally sometimes. We all do).

However, there is a big difference between recognizing that you screwed up, resolving to move on and getting stuck thinking that if you had just done or said that perfect thing, it would all be different.

The key to continuing to date in a healthy way (whether it's with your ex or not), is to be able to shorten the cycle between relationship blowup, recognizing what needed to change or be different and then trying again.

The difference between a big realization, ie, "I cheated and turned this into a giant mess, that was a huge mistake" and obsession, is that obsession usually focuses on a few trivial details. For example, what you said during the breakup.

The finer details were not the problem.

I promise, getting stuck on your hair color, or whether you

should have said or done some specific thing differently does not serve you in the long run. It's also a good way to derail yourself and get stuck in the past.

So if you're telling yourself a story about why you broke up, I challenge you to drop the story. Let it go. Resolve to do better next time and mend bridges, but don't stay stuck.

Thought Catalog, it's a website.

www.thoughtcatalog.com

Social

facebook.com/thoughtcatalog
twitter.com/thoughtcatalog
tumblr.com/thoughtcatalog
instagram.com/thoughtcatalog

Corporate

www.thought.is

79134650R00061

Made in the USA
San Bernardino, CA
12 June 2018